Geoff Page grew up on a cattle station on the Clarence River, NSW. He is based in Canberra and has published twenty-two collections of poetry as well as two novels and five verse novels. His recent books include *Improving the News* (Pitt Street Poetry 2013), *New Selected Poems* (Puncher & Wattmann 2013) and *Gods and Uncles* (Pitt Street Poetry 2015). He also edited *The Best Australian Poems 2014* and *The Best Australian Poems 2015* (Black Inc).

PLEVNA

A biography in verse

Sir Charles 'Plevna' Ryan (1853–1926)

GEOFF PAGE

UWA PUBLISHING

First published in 2016 by
UWA Publishing
Crawley, Western Australia 6009
www.uwap.uwa.edu.au

UWAP is an imprint of UWA Publishing
a division of The University of Western Australia

THE UNIVERSITY OF
WESTERN
AUSTRALIA

ISBN: 9781742588209

A full CIP data entry is available from
the National Library of Australia

Cover design by Upside Creative
Typeset in Bembo by Lasertype
Printed by McPherson's Printing Group

Cover images: H00483 and P01732.001
from the Australian War Memorial (cropped).

He refused to take chloroform, and I took his leg off above the knee without any anaesthetic. He never said a word, and went on smoking his cigarette all the time. When the captain came round with his notebook afterwards to take down the name, age, and regiment of each wounded man, my patient answered all the questions quietly and unconcernedly while I was stitching up the flap of skin over the stump.

Maudlin to address the dead,
especially unintroduced,
but even so, Charles Ryan,
I have the urge to do so,
Melbourne surgeon, later Sir,
but 'Charlie' to your friends.
Also known as 'Plevna' Ryan
but that can wait till later.

Your dates are 1853
to 1926,
a life as long as mine is now
or was when I began.
Why have we no biography,
three hundred pages, dense with footnotes,
boasting your achievements?
That book would praise the patients saved,
one of them Ned Kelly,
and lift you just a little from
the spreading silence that begins
when all who've known us have in turn
succumbed to their extinction.

Your book in 1897,
assisted by your friend, John Sandes,
leaves a vivid whiff
but covers two years only.
Those stiffened, glass-protected birds
that sometimes spooked your patients
are no less silent now;
most probably in landfill somewhere.
The sounds of upper Collins Street
around your century's turn,
the clip-clop on macadam,
the hurrying of ladies' heels
and grind of cable trams
have not survived in sepia.

Those corpses at Gallipoli
(that both sides paused nine hours to bury
and you to photograph)
are just a little closer.

The Russian guns though back at Plevna
were each day rich with stench and colour.
Two chapters of a daughter's memoir
sedately offer more.
The minutes from those Melbourne meetings
do not supply what we require.
Your laughter would not fit inside
their curlicues of longhand.

It struck the lattice of a window, and at once exploded. When I rushed in, the ward was full of dust and smoke, out of which came terrible screams and cries. Four of the patients had been killed on the spot, and seven others had been horribly wounded.

1853,
September 20, war
in the Crimea poised
and you are born on Killeen station,
a cottage done in pisé
not too far from Longwood in
Her Majesty's Victoria.

Your father, Charles, an Irishman,
an overlander down from Sydney;
your mother, Marian, a Cotton,
family with English substance.
The details though elude us:
the towels, the heated water,
and who the midwife was.

Within a year or so your father,
deciding to give up his lease,
re-locates to Brighton with
a view out on the bay and starts
his stock-and-station business,
more viable from Melbourne.
Later, you grow up in Richmond
and, later still, Mount Macedon.
Your father's vast, obsessive garden
runs to more than twenty acres
with foreign trees and eucalypts
and shrubs from round the world —
until the 1890s 'bust'
forces him to sell.

We read about your sister, Ellis —
the future Mrs Ellis Rowan,
traveller and wild flower painter.
Melbourne in the 1860s
is swelling from the goldfields still
and pastoral supplies are needed.
Ergo: Ryan & Hammond.

Enough to pay for Melbourne Grammar,
just a youthful school back then,
where, plainly, you apply yourself
and aren't without some humour.
There'd be a photo of your classmates
that I have not yet seen.
Your father works — and dreams a bit.
Your mother reins him in.
Your wife would do the same for you.
Your daughter, much much later,
calls her grandma 'firm and fierce'.
Unfair perhaps but just.
A hierarchy of siblings
proliferates around you.
One sister weds an admiral
and vanishes to England.

Who knows where the surgeon comes from?
Likewise, your love for birds?
Your knowledge of photography?
Its lenses and its fixers
supply a sort of clue.
Altruism plays a part
but not, I think, *noblesse oblige*.
The colony's too young for that.

Already at the Grammar
the scions of the Western District
are more or less content
to work their not-long-stolen acres
and watch the price of wool.
We know you're wanting more than this
but, even so, the Med School
must surely be a shock;
the way a scalpel slices in
to spill things on a slab
and how a ribcage may be sawn
to offer up its thoughts.

I doubt though you are one of those
who, first day in Anatomy,
step outside to vomit.

Those black cattle, however, that are found along the banks of the Danube are almost amphibious and they take to the water like dogs. As soon as the front files had taken to the water the others followed them readily, and the Circassians followed in the boats, rounding up the stragglers with their whips, and towing their horses, re-equipped with the pigskin lifebelts, behind them. So in darkness and rain, across the hurrying flood of the Danube they brought four hundred head of Roumanian cattle, and left behind them two dead sentries lying with their faces turned towards the sky.

Five years, not four, the course is then,
one year more than Britain.
Fifty students, give or take,
with lectures on Anatomy
given by Professor Halford,
St Andrews graduate,
down here in the colonies
and getting the vocation started.

The text books are all leather bound
and stored away in glass.
Their grotesque instances
on Parkville afternoons
detain you after lectures..

Somewhere there'd be talk of Thales,
the Hippocratic oath declaring:
'First, one does no harm'.
You have a feel for detail surely,
that much can be assumed,
but also intuition.
Later you will make your name
for quick-fire diagnoses.

Setting bones in those days is
a sort of carpentry;
and sutures done with gut,
a wifely kind of sewing.
You learn the feel of stainless steel,
the clamps and forceps, graded blades,
and hacksaws for the bones.

Each morning, one stop in from Richmond,
you catch the tram up Swanston Street
in every sort of weather.
And, sometimes, after classes,
you drink, but not excessively,
with colleagues at a Carlton pub,

or so we must imagine,
the smell of formalin
persistent in your clothes.

The Melbourne School of Medicine
is still too small and embryonic.
Your high ambition's needing more,
a final year at Edinburgh
where medicine has deeper roots
and fosters innovation.

It too proves not enough.
You move to Bonn and then Vienna —
all that Europe has to offer
and not yet twenty-three.

While I was making my way up to the left of our line, I saw three Turkish artillerymen lying dead. One had been shot in the abdomen, and presented a terrible spectacle with his intestines all hanging out. The two others had had their legs carried away by shells.

The *Wanderjahr*, the *Wanderjahr* —
with *Poste restante* remittances
from father Charles in stock & station.
Norway, Sweden, Paris, Bonn
(the clinic of Professor Busch),
Vienna on the *Blaue Donau*;
then westward through Bavaria
and, finally, to Rome.

You're sitting in a café there
with friend, García C——,
youthful surgeon, would-be poet
'improvident in money matters'.
He owes you quite a sum by now.
You're at a 'low financial ebb'
and, 'glancing idly at The Times',
suddenly you see it,
the ad for twenty British surgeons
to serve the Ottomans,
currently a little stirred
by problematic Serbs.
Two hundred pounds a year, it says,
paid each month in gold.
The interview's in London though.
It's time to foreclose on García,
to cash your friend's gold watch,
his heirloom from Castile,
for 'twenty-five napoleons'.
Upset, he hands you just enough
to get to Neuchâtel
and check the *Poste restante*.

Luckily, your money's there.
You hurry on to London where
the Ottoman ambassador
is busy, so you see his son
and wave your Edinburgh credentials.

Two days more and you are off
by stages for Constantinople;
pause again at old Vienna;
then sail on down the Danube.
On board there are some English doctors;
'a number of pretty Roumanian women'.
It proves 'a jolly party'.
You disembark at Rustchuk
and take the train to Varna where
you catch a little steamer,
half-day to Istanbul.
It 'rises from the Bosphorus',
your 'dreams at last fulfilled'.

And twenty years or so from here
you'll write down how it was:
its 'mosques and minarets',
its 'dark green cypress groves',
its 'towers of gleaming marble',
those 'gilded pinnacles'.

Those flashes of fire were the last things he ever saw on earth, for one of the shells struck him full in the face and took his head clean off. There was a spirting from the blood-vessels in the neck, and then the headless corpse spun around in a circle, the legs moving convulsively like those of a chicken when its throat is cut. I was so close to the man that I could see every movement, and the sight affected my nerve centres in the way that the normal system is affected by any sudden and horrible sight; that is to say, I turned cold all over and was very sick on the spot.

Army Surgeon = Major.
You have a week or so, you're told,
before you front the Serbs.
You leave the Misserie's Hotel
and move into the barracks.
Each day, you're free to be a tourist
and still you're only twenty-three.
It's all so overwhelming if
you're 'fresh from Melbourne' which,
some 'forty years before',
was just, as you are quick to add,
a 'camping-ground for blacks'.

You climb, while sweating just a little,
the 'tower of the Seraskierat',
relishing the view:
the Black Sea and the Marmora,
the Bosphorus, the Dardanelles.
The weather, we assume, is good.
You don't say otherwise.
From there, you see Scutari where
rows of English officers
not too dissimilar to you
are twenty-three years buried.
You muse on Florence Nightingale
and maybe just a moment on
the papers you have signed.

You're struck by how the city
by day is 'colour, life and brightness'
and then, by night, 'appalling',
unlit, deserted save by dogs,
which do not need excuses
to trap you in an alley.

You miss the well-lit *trottoirs*
of Paris and Vienna.

Like any tourist you
are quick to sample the bazaars,
smiling at the 'solemn Turks'
who swindle with 'polite decorum'.
You're smiling at the 'three-day Sundays',
the way each follows in its turn,
Muslim, Jewish, Christian.
Another day, you're visiting
the picnic spot they call 'Sweet Waters',
marvelling at 'wealthy Turks'
who wheel their harem out in 'yashmaks',
their carriages as well-appointed
as any seen in Hyde Park, London,
or in the *bois* of Paris.
Once or twice, you hire *caïques*
that ply the Golden Horn.
You are a Turkish major but
you're also a *Giaour*,
a foreigner who can not pray —
or does not pray correctly.

I see you stroll the streets with colleagues
awaiting their appointments too.
Your habits are convivial
and yet you are content alone,
pondering your rendezvous
with shellfire up ahead.

How often do you wish that you
might be at home already
with 'rooms' in upper Collins,
consoling well-off matrons
or disconcerted gents
with scribbled-down placebos
that do less harm than good?

But, no, it's much too soon for that.
Experience is what you need.

I stitched it up and washed the wound; but the case was a hopeless one. If I could have given him chloroform, thoroughly opened him up, and washed everything out, I might have been able to save him; but there was no time for that. He lingered on in great agony, and died on the following day.

One week more, you've got your orders:
regimental surgeon with
a fresh eight hundred men
and twenty-seven officers;
the privates, conscripts from Kyrchehir,
away in Asia Minor.
They're 'all well clothed',
'grand specimens' and each one with his
new Martini rifle.

You travel slowly north by train,
bivouacking at the stations.
Along the route you get your 'charger',
'grey stallion', 'powerful animal'.
You're bound for Nish. It's June and dusty.
They bring your first malingerer.
You have a mind to make up quickly.
It's done — they need to know
you will not be imposed upon.
He's sent back to the rear and given
'a round three dozen with a stick'
across the buttocks. No more cases.

The troops are off the train and marching,
five days to Sofia.
The route you take is 'mountainous'
but 'very picturesque'.
The 'insects of Bulgaria'
establish they're unequalled for
'ferocity' and 'size'.

Finally, you reach Sofia
and quote a line from Tennyson:
it sparkled like a grain of salt.
Better from a distance though.
You're learning Turkish from
your friend called Mehmet Ali
who points at things around the tent

and makes you say their name.
Already you've acquired some basics:
'*Dilli nitchika*' — 'Put out your tongue'.
You comment too, in passing, on
how reasonably Turks treat Bulgars
who, reasonably, hate them back.

It's also in Sofia that
you first attend a female patient.
'The hand was small and finely formed'
and offered through a curtain.
You wisely offer no prescription.
You ride on up to Pirot,
camping in the hills
and managing a few hours off
for potting ducks and hares.

Then, at last, it's Nish.
Headquarters, Turkish Army.
You're drafted to the hospital
and life proves serious.
A Turkish soldier's wounded knee
necessitates an amputation.
Your first. He takes no chloroform;
makes not a sound and smokes
a cigarette throughout.

It bored a hole clean through the upper portion of the brain; but the sufferer, though he was weak from loss of blood, was perfectly rational. I put a syringe into the orifice, and cleaned the lacerated portion of the brain with a solution of carbolic, afterwards dressing the skull with an antiseptic pad and bandages. The man was put into the hospital, where he remained for about six weeks, and at the end of that time he was discharged cured.

December now; an armistice;
the Serbs have given up.
You head back to Sofia,
following your regiment
by pony through the snow.

The English surgeons hatch a plan
for putting on a Christmas dinner
when suddenly you're on your way
to Orkhanieh to guard the passes.
Here, it's neither Serb nor Russian
but dysentery that does the damage,
you yourself a victim too.

Five weeks more, you're off to Widdin,
up there in Bulgaria's
vulnerable north-western corner.
The Danube is a mile-wide border
slipping swiftly by.
Thirty thousand Turkish troops
are digging in to stop the Russians,
expected any day
to sweep down through Roumania
which holds, in turn, the fortress town
called Kalafat across the river.

It bristles with artillery.
Dysentery and lung disease,
malaria as well,
are less dramatic than the guns,
emplaced in handy range
and waiting for a nod from Moscow.

It's Widdin too where Doctor Black,
that drunken Englishman and surgeon,
is prone to firing his revolver
at all who cause him small annoyance.

Eventually, the Turks,
embarrassed and impatient,
supply him with a sweet ten pounds
and bundle him upriver on
a steamer for Belgrade.

More impressive is the ball
Commander Osman Pasha stages
to celebrate the recent peace
and fund his hospitals.
Your friend, Effendi, German-trained
and rather dapper, has contrived
a ballroom of attractive ladies:
Bulgarians and Spanish,
'seventeen to twenty years
of age' with 'rich dark hair'.

You call yourself a 'dancing man'
as Turkish officers are sitting
'cross-legged' on divans,
more used to paying for a dancer
than doing it themselves.
You think about that ball in Brussels
preceding Waterloo.
'I gave myself up to the business of pleasure
with all the ardour of two and twenty,'
you boast, much later, in a pair
of accidental anapæsts —
though really you are twenty-four.
'The champagne corks were popping
as thickly as the bullets later'.

It's April, spring, the twenty-fourth
and sundry diplomats ensure
that war's declared once more.
Even so, you manage lunch
with two Roumanian officers,
stepping off at your hotel

down there by the Danube,
one a Captain Georgione
who, following a lengthy meal,
invites you back to Kalafat.

Next day, equipped with British passport,
you dress in 'mufti' ('English Tweed')
arrange a locum, hire two rowers
and head across the river.
Roumanian Customs 'frank' you through
though not without suspicion.
You meet, almost at once,
with Captain Georgione —
stay on for lunch and dinner,
talking German mainly,
regaling them with details
of Widdin's troops and guns,
magnified by two or three,
and smiling at your talent for
some light mendacities.
By dawn, you're with your pair of boatmen.
At six, you're back at the hotel.
No one is, it seems,
'the wiser for my escapade'.

It's Widdin where you finally
are fired upon in anger.
The batteries at Kalafat
drop a shell through your hotel,
unpleasantly truncating lunch
with Colonel Stracey, entertaining
Englishman, who's lately been
consorting with the Russians.
The two of you head back to town.
The barrage lasts three hours.
Later, 'four or five' are waiting,
wounded in the hospital.

It's proving inconvenient.
'Stracey and I had nothing to eat.
The butchers and bakers in Widdin
were down in their cellars and no
amount of money would
induce them to come out.'

It was a beautiful summer night, with moon and stars shining, as I walked back to my quarters utterly fagged out with that tremendous day's work. A couple of miles away to the north I could see the long ridge of the Janik Bair shining in the moonlight. More than a thousand Turks and more than one thousand two hundred Russians lay stretched on the other side of the hill, and along the line of the fighting from Bukova on the left to Grivitza on the right.

The Russians though are moving quickly.
Widdin is of little use.
July 14, you all set out
for Krivodol and then,
with just a few hours' pause,
you're part of an advance guard on
the forced march up to Plevna,
the town that later will supply
the nickname you'll enjoy back home.

Footsore, running short of water,
three hundred soldiers falling out,
the men each day have just two biscuits,
a drop or two of water.
July 18, you get to Plevna.
And find a Turkish bath first off;
then 'sally' out to check the town.
It's not so small. Eight mosques, two churches.
Seventeen thousand people
lived there at the start
although, you're quick to note,
the rich have left already.

Except, it seems, for Dr Robert,
 presumably pronounced 'Robaire',
born at Neuchâtel
and now a 'fashionable physician'
(as you yourself will live to be)
doing well in this small corner
of the Turkish empire.
His housekeeper's a Viennese
and wondrous in the kitchen.
Your fellow doctor, Weinberger,
and you are asked to dinner.
You drink off several bottles of
the not-bad local wine
and listen to Robert, in German,
recount his 'amatory exploits'

way back in his student days
with 'detail that was edifying'.
Who knows what use you put it to?
Afterwards, he plays piano,
'thumping' on the keys,
roaring 'ditties' from the French,
the German and Bulgarian
in praise of *Wein, Weib und Gesang.*

Next morning, unabashed,
you ride out with Robert
to check preliminaries.
You climb a ridge and, from the top,
glimpse, just a mile away,
'the gleam of Russian bayonets' —
while salvos of their shells fall short
or rush instead straight over
and on towards the town.

You've got some dressings with you,
which quite soon come in handy
for stitching up a palm.
Half a dozen others
are well beyond such care,
missing legs, intestines spread.
A Turkish gunner, just beside you,
has his head ripped neatly off.

And seventeen or so years later,
while you are working on your memoir,
it's not become less gross.

Instead of the rows of students who usually grace these scientific ceremonies, scores of the snow-white doves that are considered sacred throughout Turkey paused now and then in their cooings, as they fluttered round the minarets of the ancient mosque above the willow grove and looked down upon the strange scene below them. The wounded soldiers took their turns each in his proper order; and as I sat on the willow stump a man with a thumb or finger, as the case might be, mangled into a shocking pulp of festering flesh, would hold up his injured hand to me as he sat on the grass at my feet, and would look on without flinching while I cut away the rotting flesh, trimmed up the place, and washed and dressed the bleeding stump that still remained. I did over a dozen of these cases in one morning; and later in the campaign, when the fighting in the redoubts began, I have amputated as many as twenty-seven fingers in succession.

Now your true work has begun:
the hospital at Plevna,
two large rooms with one for beds,
the other with some benches,
the wounded limping in by foot
or drawn in the 'arabas',
the unsprung wheels of which produce
'the most exquisite agony',
the dead and dying equally
'matted together with clotted blood'.

Later, you still store the view
of those first three you treated:
jaw destroyed, extruded liver,
intestines carried in the hands.
Is this what those uncounted hours
in Edinburgh and Parkville
had (more or less) prepared you for?

You're stunned by Turkish fortitude,
their courage under pain,
and are distressed in turn by how
they won't take alcohol to ease it.
How is it they're content to die
refusing amputation,
believing that a severed limb
might shut them out of paradise ?
You notice how the Berdan rifle
drills 'a clear hole through'
and simplifies your task somewhat.
'*Verbana su, effendi*'
your hear them crying out.
'*Verbana su, hakim bashi*'
'Give me a drink of water, doctor'.

At 3 p.m. you're given orders
to turn up at a nearby house
where work is even grimmer.

You labour on until eleven;
then walk home through the summer night,
the 'moon and stars' still shining down.

Next morning you are up at six
and back to check the wounded.
'His case was hopeless from the start,'
you note about a Russian boy.
You're ordered to a little mosque
where eighty more are waiting.
You have to start by sorting out
the living from the dead.

Extracting bullets, stitching wounds,
you move among them steadily,
allowing each, at best, ten minutes.
You note, and use no irony,
how doves fly round the minaret.
The muezzin calls the world to prayer.

You're happy to admit, years later,
'We often made … mistakes',
you and Osman, fellow surgeon,
'capable anatomist'
who learned his skills in Paris.

You tell the story also of
those twenty-seven wounded fingers
severed at a session
and how an Arab regiment
was prone to blowing off its digits
to re-achieve its village
and how when Osman Pasha sought
your verdict on a case
you brought your colleagues in to make
a hard, professional decision.
Yes, the wound was self-inflicted.

And so the hapless three
who'd blown their trigger finger off
were put before a firing squad
and hastily dispatched.

A sergeant stepped up and bandaged the eyes of the culprits, who were placed on their knees in a row a few yards distant from each other. A few moments were granted to them to say their prayers, then a naked sword-blade flashed in the sunlight, a quick word of command rang out, a volley startled the camp, and the victims fell dead riddled with bullets. It was a sharp remedy, but a sure one, and after that we had no more malingerers.

You have a feel for strategy;
are quick to understand
the barrages and fusillades
that bring your patients in.
You know the dispositions.
A map is there inside your head.
From time to time, you're free
to ride out to emplacements where
you take a closer look.
A doctor's kit provides excuse.

You talk of the Circassians,
brave and ruthless, born to steal,
who, back at Widdin, robbed a mob
of cattle from Roumanians
and swam them back across the Danube.
Here, in Plevna, they're like vultures
preying on the Russian dead,
selling off their valuables
next day at the bazaar.
You buy a signet ring yourself
which features Aesculapius,
first man of your noble calling.
Osman Pasha disapproves
and one night five of them are caught
rummaging among the dead.
He has them hanged at dawn
'*pour encourager les autres.*'

There's now a sort of ten-day truce
between the first and second battles.
You ride with Robert to the hills
and watch them burying the dead,
the Russians and the Turkish
always kept distinct. 'The Moslem
will not sleep with the *Giaour*,
even in the grave.'

Later, you get closer;
stir a body with your scabbard
and see the 'swarms of noxious creatures'
busy underneath.

You're boarding with a Bulgar now,
a landlord whom you pay no rent;
he has a very pretty daughter
with just one word of English, 'London',
which she offers rather often.
You relish her 'coquettish glance'
but things, we must assume from here,
do not go any further.

The hospitality of Doctor
Robert still continues:
the songs, the drinking, the cuisine,
the wondrous Viennese.
Later, when you've long left Plevna,
you hear that Doctor Robert,
thought to be a Russophile,
was, while the siege was still in place,
condemned and shot for spying.

It's still July and on the
morning of the thirtieth
the second Plevna battle starts.
You finish at the hospital
and ride up to the front,
sword, revolver, doctor's kit,
to see what might transpire.
You meet your friend, the Polish prince,
Michael Czetwertinski,
who heads the general's bodyguard
(but that's a different story).

And suddenly you find yourself,
encouraged by your colonel,
galloping with Czetwertinski
pursuing fleeing Russians.
You're charging through a field of barley
when all at once the Russians see
you're just a group of eighty
and stop to hold their ground.
You turn about and scamper
flat-out for your lines,
their bullets buzzing all about you,
riders pitching from their horses.

Your turnabout has spooked the Turkish
infantry who flee as well
till Osman and his staff
start shooting down the first to run.
You canter (shame-faced?) back to work,
knowing there'll be plenty of it,
and later on you hear
the Russians lost a quarter of their force,
seven thousand dead,
the Turks a mere eight hundred.
And so the second battle ends.

In many places a foot, a finger, or a hand protruding from the ground revealed the presence of the dead; and as I advanced farther down into the valley from the Turkish line of defence, I came across a great number of bodies which had escaped the notice of the burial parties altogether. There they lay, with the hot July sun beating down upon them, and the cool moisture of the earth teeming with horrible living things beneath them.

You find a second Bulgar's house,
a 'strange, two-storey edifice',
right beside the Tutchenitza.
Understandably, they're not
particularly friendly.
You occupy the upper floor.
His garden is astonishing,
'asters, zineas, balsams'.
You post some sample seeds to Melbourne
and, after almost twenty years,
pluck the 'lineal descendants'
of those that bloomed when you lived on
the 'bloodstained soil of Plevna'.

And this is no hyperbole.
The Tutchenitza floods and brings
a human head, its 'teeth set fast
in a horrid grin'. Turkish? Russian?
You bury it beneath a bush
and two days later check
the battlefield. You find a gully
full of Russian heads and think
of those Circassians,
so prone to cutting throats
when scavenging the wounded.
Ahmet though, your own
Circassian, has always been
your faithful servant, even if
he won't go near a pig
no matter who gives orders.

August 31,
you suddenly hear guns
and canter to the front
where soon you're cutting bullets loose
(nineteen in a mere three hours)
and use no chloroform.

You ride on even closer,
right into the 'thick of it'.
You see your friend, the Polish prince —
who's had his big black charger
shot away beneath him.
'A perfect storm of shot and shell'
delivered by the Russians
sees you trying to extract
a pair of wounded Turks from what
the Russians have in store for them.
'Caught between two fires',
you prop them on your horse
and lose one on the way.
You snatch the other through to safety,
receiving 'not a scratch'.
Set up at a clearing station
and working with the wounded,
you stay till six o'clock.

It's been a rotten day for Turkey.
Thirteen hundred killed
for 'absolutely nothing'.
Not much better is the dash
they make to raise the siege of Lovtcha.
Starting late, and potted at
by Cossacks on the way,
you're part of Osman Pasha's force
which, hearing now that Lovtcha's gone,
moves forward and encounters
'four hundred Turks all lying dead
and fearfully disfigured'.
Two days on, you're back in Plevna,
thinned somewhat but ready for
the third and final battle.

"I saw him lying there before me," whispered my patient to me as I dressed his wounds, "and the impulse to kill him came into my mind. I suppose he read my purpose in my face, for he pointed to his wound, and then he held up his hands to me as if to ask for quarter. As I crawled over on my hands and knees, I knelt over him and pointed to my own wounds in reply. Then I drew my revolver and shot him through the head."

September 7. Third time round.
The Russians bring up 90,000;
the Turks a third of that.
Day One has you ride out promptly
just to have a glance.
And then, for several lengthy days,
you're sweating at your trade.

A few days later you are at
the tough redoubt of Krishin when
the Turkish line begins to split.
You 'shout', 'entreat' and 'threaten' but
the fire is just too hot.
You meet your Polish friend again.
Together, you upbraid them but
eventually you flee as well.
Cantering to Plevna, you
observe the Turks in flight
'like sheep before a bushfire',
the Russians just a half mile off.

That night the Turks attempt a come-back,
stalled by 'murderous fire'
from Russian Krenke/Berdan rifles.
Next morning you have fifteen hundred
extra wounded in the square.
You do the best you can
and get away at 3 p.m.
to see the Turks send off the Russians.
Years later, back in Melbourne,
you still smile at that Russian phrase:
'It was decided to abandon …'

A certain to and fro continues;
and now your team's acquired
four thousand extra wounded.
Your forty doctors, uncomplaining,
work a twenty-four hour shift.

The waiting list is four days long;
the food, at least, is adequate.
You note also that Osman Pasha
strides among the wounded,
offering a doughty comfort.

The sun's been hard for days.
Some officers on either side
are deputised to start a cease-fire
for burying the bodies which
are equally offensive to
both Ottoman and Russian nostrils.
They parley there in 'no man's land'
but cannot reach accord.
They share a brandy at the finish,
refused by Tewfik Bey,
accepted by the Pole.

The stink persists; the war goes on.
You canter out at three
for coffee and a cigarette
with old friend, Sadik Pasha,
secure in his redoubt which needs
a sudden dash of thirty yards
through heavy fire to gain its safety.
One day, the man who holds your horse
is neatly cut in two by one
half-errant Russian shell.

Favoured by Mustafa Bey,
you ride out on reconnaissance,
ready with your Winchester —
an instrument Hippocrates
might well have had his doubts about.
Fourteen hours in all you spend
in various pursuits and flights
and still your life is charmed.

The siege has moved to winter now;
supplies are running low.
Your reinforcement stocks
of bandages and drugs
are carried off by Russians.
The road is open; then cut off.

You get your friend, the Polish prince,
now sick with dysentery,
away towards Sofia.
Much later, when the peace is made,
he'll lunch with Skobeleff,
the famous Russian victor, who
will cheerfully remind him that
had I ever 'captured you
I would have had you shot, of course.'

Seeing that the soldier in the trenches nearest to us was puffing calmly at a cigarette himself in the intervals of business, Czetwertinski sang out to him, "Verbana a-tish," meaning, "Give me a light." The man clambered out of the trench, saluted, and handed his lighted cigarette to Prince Czetwertinksi. As he stood there in the act of saluting a rifle bullet went through his head, and the man threw up his hands and fell dead.

Your life's become a struggle now
with 'wounds, waste, filth, disease and death'.
Your hospital is two large rooms;
'the white-washed walls were splashed with blood'
and you the only surgeon.
The 'antiseptic dressings'
are now completely used.
You're scraping maggots from the wounds
and watch your patients 'die by inches'.

 In your book, years later, you
retain those memories in detail,
the 'gangrened legs', the 'shoulders smashed',
the problems faced with amputation.
Smallpox, then the typhoid fever
progressively appear;
with body lice to add annoyance.

Each morning at the garden gate
outside your hospital, a row
of new-laid corpses greets you,
faces you had known and talked with;
stories of their villages
scattered through the Empire.

Abruptly, unexpectedly,
you yourself are wounded;
your luck's not absolute, it seems.
You're cantering to see a friend,
the hardy Sadik Pasha,
when suddenly from nowhere lobs
a random Russian shell
exploding just behind you.
A minor scrap of shrapnel
gets you in the neck.
It's like 'a piece of red-hot iron'
though just a 'surface wound'.

It won't impede your work although
you do admit about this time
to feeling just a tad 'despondent'.
And back in Melbourne you'll concede
that 'even now I lie awake' with
'curdled blood' and 'stifled moans'.

Then, all at once, the road is open.
Chefket Pasha's done his work.
Several British surgeons,
some of them your former colleagues,
arrive with the relief.
You ask them round to supper and
the hubbub's all in English.
They're sent by Stafford House,
the British charity,
to tend the wounded Turks.

There is a contretemps, however.
Osman Pasha has declared
the injured will be better off
away down in Sofia,
despite the days of broken roads.
lying in between.
The new arrivals are incensed;
this isn't what they came for.
They call it 'barbarous' and 'brutal'
but you agree with Osman Pasha
and tell your story later in
the London Times, complete with detail,
to set the record straight.

Once you ride out with your friends
to show them what you know about
the famed redoubts and recent battles.
And draw a sudden salvo down
upon your recklessness.

'Luckily, all four of us
came out of it without a scratch.'
Your neck wound though is getting worse,
a 'suppurating cavity'.
With all these reinforcements, you
apply to take some leave of absence.
Your mother Marian's in London.
Your contract spelt out one year only;
it's almost eighteen months.
You make it plain that you'll be back
(not knowing that the siege will end
a few weeks further on).
Doctor Robert puts on supper,
complete with 'patriotic songs
in half a dozen languages',
and next day you are off,
riding with the wounded
headed for Sofia.

You're up the front but even there
you hear the groaning from the road,
the rub of bone on bone.
The dead are left 'to soak in rain'
or 'bleach beneath the sun'.
It's hard; you're sick but finally
you're safely in the city; you reach Sofia
where, you tell the Argus later,
you notice 'three Bulgarians
hanged in the street. They simply tie
their hands and feet and haul them up,
death being caused by asphyxia.'
This episode's not in the book.
A few days more, Constantinople.

Then old Mustapha Bey waved his sword, and sang out to me to come with them; so I forgot that I was a simple medical officer. I drove the spurs into my horse, and in half a minute I was riding alongside Czetwertinski in a wild charge against the flying Russians. We climbed the hill at a gallop, rode through our own men at the top, and charged down the slope towards Schahoffskoi's fugitives.

You're back at Misserie's Hotel;
'clean sheets' and 'French cuisine';
first you've had in fifteen months.
You get out to the clubs and cafés
where everyone, it seems, requires
the latest news of Plevna.

You visit the Seraskierat
and find you're warmly thanked
although you cannot help but note
the swell of Turkish losses was
no fault of Osman Pasha's.

You've written to your mother and
expect her quick reply.
The city, you can't help but see,
is dense with young adventurers
(not unlike yourself),
some more plausible than others,
deluded con-men, 'sterling fellows'
and many in between.

One day you're in a party which
steams out to see the 'British squadron',
riding thoughtfully at anchor.
You meet a 'Mr Wrench' who helps you
track down your outstanding pay.
Byzantium to Istanbul,
he knows how things have always worked.
In just a few short days
it's all paid up in 'silver coin'.
'I had to get a small hand-barrow'
to carry it away.

You shift into a club and meet
a range of free, 'congenial spirits'.
With them you haunt the *cafés chantants*.

You hear a French girl sing of Plevna
and while she's still in flight on stage
you're forced to take a bow
when someone points you out and names you
hero of the siege.

You're waiting still to hear from mother
(and planning to get back to Plevna)
when suddenly you're told
the town's cut off completely now
and ready to surrender.

The Stafford House Committee
has offered you, some days before,
good terms to work at Erzeroum,
a mountain town in Asia Minor
whose Turks are likewise under pressure.
The place is 'full of wounded men'.
Medical supplies are needed.
The London trip to see your mother
will have to be deferred.

Your friends put on a farewell dinner
quickly at the club.
'Bumpers of champagne' are sunk
by men who know, too well, just how
'a fever or a rifle-bullet'
can mean they'll meet no more.
And in the early morning hours
they see you to the quay.

You board a little steamer
and happily discover
its 'fine old Frenchman' captain keeps
his 'knowledge of gastronomy'.
The small boat makes a tourist's circle;
you call at several ports along
the Black Sea's northern edge

and land at last at Trebizond
to find a 'good hotel'.

Next morning though, you're off at once
to climb to Erzeroum with just
emergency supplies;
the rest must come along more slowly.
You press on up the road
that Xenophon 'two thousand years
ago had travelled with his legions'.
It's redolent with Greek allusions
but, strangely, in reverse;
he marched down and *you* ride up.
Do you think of what awaits you?
His famous cry of 'Thalassa!'
is what you leave behind.

A few moments before, while we were galloping forwards against the fugitives, I felt as brave as a lion; but when once I had turned my back to them and heard their bullets whistling round me, a mortal dread came over me, and if I had had a hundred millions in the bank I would have given it all to be a furlong farther from the muzzles of those Russian rifles.

The way at first is 'picturesque'.
The four of you are riding horses,
'badly broken brutes'.
The local Turks impress you:
'hardy as the mountain ash'.
You side with those inclined to think
these valleys and ravines were once
'the cradle of the human race'.

Higher up, the second night
you come out on a plateau
and stop at Ghumish Kané,
a small town mining silver.
With just a little *baksheesh* you
put up at its *hamman*,
'well steamed' and sleeping on divans.

Next evening, you're at Baiburt
which 'sleeps on in the present,
dreaming of the past.'
One day more, you're higher up
among 'giant rhododendrons' and
the ruins of successive castles.

By now it's 'seven thousand feet'.
You see the great Euphrates and
surmise you're nearing 'Eden';
then hear by local telegraph
that Erzeroum has fallen —
which proves untrue when you arrive
next day at 5 p.m.

Three surgeons only still remain;
you move into their 'great bare house',
sleeping on the floor.
The town has mountains all around;
it's also 'picturesque'.

Population: 40,000,
Turkish and Armenian.
You're introduced to Mukhtar Pasha,
very much the man-in-charge;
then organise the hospital,
hire some *jarra bashis*
to do the bandaging.

Three hundred beds, you count in all;
each covered with a Persian quilt
which, with a good supply of light,
appears to make 'a garden
full of flowers' although
the wounded wear a paler colour.

It's late November now.
The death rate's trending down,
six a week from your three hundred,
but soon a single typhus case
brings memories of Plevna.

The snow falls early in December
and now you've got four thousand
'sick and wounded in the town'.
Your stores from Trebizond arrive,
delayed by weather on the road.
Your team is working well, although
pyaemia, pneumonia,
along with typhus are
working full-time for the Russians.
It's minus forty Fahrenheit.
The Russian general, Melikoff,
has meanwhile taken Kars
and, feeling incommoded, sends
his wounded Turks to Erzeroum,
struggling through the snow.

Two thousand men set off;
three hundred, more or less, arrive
with frostbite added to their wounds.
Gangrene now as well
is common in the wards —
and doctors aren't immune to typhus.
One, hallucinating wildly,
 is sent to Trebizond.

To cheer yourselves a little you
devise a plan for Christmas Dinner.
'All the European doctors'
are cordially invited.
Mr Zohrab, British Consul,
kindly lends his house.
To add an 'English touch'
your friends and you suggest plum pudding;
then whip it up yourselves,
boiling it all night, 'a viscous,
cedematous mass'.
Next day you wheel it in with leaping
tongues of brandy flame.
It's seriously inedible.
First and last time *you* attempt
the cooking of dessert.
You get through most of Mr Zohrab's
well-stocked cellar though
before you leave at dawn.

Within a fortnight most of you
are 'down with typhus'. In a month
'more than half were dead'.
Pinkerton, your surgeon friend,
takes two long weeks to fade away.
Two hundred soldiers die each day
from illness — not the Russians.

On January 8
you're coming down yourself
while cobbling up a crate
to bury Pinkerton.
A fortnight later on you learn
that Denniston, your other friend,
has meanwhile run, without assistance,
the whole damned show himself.

Turkish burial parties had already been out burying our dead; but the Russians were left where they fell. Nearly all of them were absolutely naked, for the Bashi-Bazouks had been there already and stripped them of arms and clothing completely.

By now it's February;
the snow's receding just a little;
the mountains though are holding theirs.
Twelve days you've been delirious.
You totter out to see the town,
a 'veritable pesthouse'.
Denniston has saved your skin —
although phlebitis in a leg
will trouble you for life.

Half the staff of twenty-seven
have fallen to the 'scourge of typhus'.
The dead lie spread in melting snow,
soldiers and civilians both.
There's not the strength to bury them
and yet the sky is clear and blue
with just a trace of cloud.
Stoker and Stivens, doctor friends,
have struggled up from Trebizond,
labouring through snowy passes,
bearing new supplies.
When guides demur at avalanches,
the doctors still press on.
Medical and British flags
persuade the Cossacks not to shoot
when Grand Duke Michael, courtesy
a timely telegram,
gives them right of way.
They stagger into Erzeroum
with quite a deal of what is needed.

The situation's looking up.
Along with Denniston and Stoker
you treat Armenians for nothing,
including their archbishop who
insists you take, in recompense,
an ancient Persian bracelet
rescued from the time of Xerxes.

Did its maker's father fight
at Salamis or Marathon?
you cannot help but wonder.

The rumour has developed that,
with Kars and Plevna gone,
the Turks will sue for peace.
One day, with great surprise, you see
two Russian officers in town,
declaring how the armistice
requires that Erzeroum must now
be occupied by Russia.
Two days later, Melikoff
arrives without a shot.

Hospitably, you ask
four Red Cross Russian doctors
to stay for dinner and the night.
They're more than happy to agree,
given what they've been through.
The meal goes well, except
the French with which you have to struggle
is nothing more than schoolboy and
produces a *faux pas* which has
the Russians calling for a duel.
You send out for a local who,
with more correct *français* contrives,
to solve the small impasse.

Your friends and you, re-horsed by Cossacks,
attend the victory parade.
'A clear, exhilarating day,'
you will remember later.
If wars are to be lost then this
is probably the way to do it.
Massed bands announce the Russian anthem;
a priest declares, with heat,

'the soldiers of the cross' again
have slain the 'infidel'.
Which leaves you unimpressed.
Several carts of wine arrive.
The 'champions of Christendom'
begin a 'glorious carouse'.

Your book will, later on, observe
the over-reach of Russia in
the treaty signed at San Stefano
and how the Congress of Berlin,
via Bismarck and the British,
will pressure Russia back a notch
and bring about a 'peace with honour'.

Meanwhile though, it's back to work.
Two thousand men in hospital
and nowhere left to send them;
Armenians, as well,
are needing your attention.
Perversely though, the Turkish wounded
are told by Istanbul to leave.
You know that most of them will die.
In bad French, on a piece of foolscap,
you send to Melikoff for help,
to have him see good sense
but in return, you're scolded for
bad paper and worse French.

After work, the Consulate
becomes a kind of club
and Mr Zohrab's helpful cellar
is cheerfully reduced
by Russian officers who've known
nothing more than snow and biscuits
these past three winter months.

You also get a telegram,
directly from the Sultan,
bestowing, for your services,
an extra decoration.
Clearly, this deserves a party.

Somewhere, deep in Erzeroum,
half a dozen of the best
Moët et Chandon are discovered,
£18 the lot.
You find, across the next few weeks,
that Russians like a drink;
Cossacks, in particular.
Officers, of course.

Other Ranks are less polite
and prone to baiting damaged Turks.
There's no sign though they rape the women.
The streets are brutal, even so.

One night, you English three
are set upon by Russian privates
and rescued, only narrowly,
by one bold Tsarist captain
flourishing a pistol.

All our operations were done out of doors in the same place under the willow tree near the bank of the Tutchenitza. A great number of cases ended fatally which in a civil hospital would probably have resulted differently; but we did not attempt any intricate operations, and we were also hampered by the fact that the patients frequently preferred to die rather than undergo the amputation of a limb. If a man had a bullet in his knee, for instance, such a thing as excising the knee or laying it open was never thought of, and we simply took the leg off.

Russians, too, in Erzeroum
are coming down with typhus,
dying off in corners,
unseen by their commanders.
You notice them while out and treating
poor Armenians;
then take it up with Pizareff,
the friendly aide-de-camp.

You meet with General Melikoff
and work beside your 'Russian confrères'
who earn your quick respect,
their troubles no less harsh than yours,
those months of frost-bite and the fevers
circling in the snow. So now,
instead of fighting Russians
you're helping them as well
and Melikoff at one point says
he'll recommend all three of you
for decorations home in Moscow
which never quite come through.
The Turkish government meanwhile
bestows an extra two.
Later, at Gallipoli,
they'll prove a talking point.

At night, you're reading Thackeray
and afterwards discover that
the candle you were using,
inserted in the nozzle of an
empty Turkish shell,
explodes in someone else's room
soon after you are gone.
Does your luck go home with you
or stay at Erzeroum?
In any case that candle
contrives to light for many years
your memories of Becky Sharp.

The situation has improved.
And now the Stafford House Committee
telegrams to bring you home,
back to Istanbul,
equipment to remain in place
for Turkish doctors staying on.

You gather your 'impedimenta',
quite notable by now,
and make your preparations for
the trip to Trebizond.
Downhill in a time of peace
should be a good deal easier
than uphill in a state of war.
You call on General Duhoffskoy
for papers and a right-of-way.
You meet his rather splendid wife,
just 'twenty years of age',
'complexion of exquisite fairness',
'large blue eyes that looked me frankly
in the face'. In eighteen months
you haven't seen a woman
anything like this.

The Bulgar girls are 'squat and swarthy';
Armenians are 'frowsy'; the Turkish
girls all 'veiled in yashmaks'.
Your heart is 'beating' with 'delight'.
You get to talk to her alone,
starting in with German,
but when you stumble she suggests
why not proceed in English?
She tells you of her trip from Tiflis,
a mere four hundred miles.
She takes an interest in your work
and listens even when you praise
the fortitude of Turks.

You talk for two hours over coffee
while her husband signs his papers
just across the room.
Back home at the Consulate,
the night before you leave,
you take down fifty books in English
from kindly Mr Zohrab's shelves
and send them as a gift.

Not all the ladies prove so charming.
Monsieur Jardin, the Paris consul,
'agreeable', 'polite', suggests
that you three gentlemen
of medicine might like
to escort down to Trebizond
'a charming Spanish widow'
marooned in Erzeroum.
Considering the other two,
you start by saying 'No'
but Monsieur Jardin is compelling
re the 'dark-eyed Spanish lady'.
Denniston and Stoker are
recruited in their turn
with French appeals to English honour
and, possibly, *noblesse oblige*.

You're mounted and about to leave
when Monsieur Jardin reappears
complete with 'Spanish lady' who's
'been beautiful in youth'
but now is somewhat less so.
And something more, an 'incubus',
an expert in complaining.
She swears in every continental
tongue except for English.
With all these languages, however,
the one thing she's not deigned to learn
is 'suffer — and be silent'.

You think perhaps of Xenophon,
his journey to the sea.
The road is long and tedious
but not without event.
Climbing through the Kodagh Pass,
a pack-horse, with your 'personal
effects', contrives to tumble to
its death four hundred feet below
and takes your many presents with it,
furs and other keepsakes
bestowed on you by Russian friends.

The *doña*, in the passes,
keeps falling from her horse,
slipping off its rear
and swearing in the snow.
At inns, if there are two rooms free,
she takes one, ensuring you
with all the other four
are wedged into the other.

You're down to timber, finally.
The pear trees that you saw in autumn
with all their golden fruit
are flowering in the spring.
Soon you sniff the Black Sea breezes.
'Trebizond at last!'

Among the flotsam and jetsam gathered there was a grisly relic from the battle-field a mile or two away. It was a human head, with most of the flesh worn off the skull by the action of the water, and the teeth set fast in a horrid grin. It was impossible to say whether it was the head of a Turk or a Russian, and I buried it under the gooseberry bush where I found it.

You go on board the 'Simois'
and steam for Istanbul.
The Spanish lady, still ill-tempered,
has blandished you to pay her way.
Not one of you complies.
Philanthropy must have its limits.
She's proved 'that rare phenomenon',
a seriously 'ungrateful woman'.

The capital, on your arrival,
is overrun with smiling Russians
camped at San Stefano. You meet
with 'Mr William Ashmead-Bartlett'
whose nephew, almost forty years
from here, will heroise the ANZACS.
With Denniston and Stoker
you write up a report
on hospitals established by
a wealthy baroness.

You meet that pretty actress — and
discreetly leave her nameless,
'La belle Américaine' —
'flashing eyes' and 'finely moulded'
but on her honeymoon, alas.
You join her picnic parties though
along the Bosphorus,
remembering the strait's 'blue waters'.
Coincidence will let you later
see her acting in La Tosca
in Melbourne's Princess Theatre.

You call on Osman Pasha too,
freed now by the Russians.
He's (understandably) 'reserved'
but gives 'a hearty welcome'.
You tell him you are soon for London
and promise him an English saddle.

In Melbourne you will gain a name
for readily bestowing gifts ...
or promising to send them.

For now though, life is in suspension
and war's still talked about.
Bismarck's Congress of Berlin
is still some months away.
You've promised Osman Pasha you'll
be back should you be needed.

A letter meanwhile has arrived
and says your mother's still in England.
You board the steamer, 'Gamboge', and,
via Smyrna, head for 'Home',
the first part of the trip improved
by fate. 'La belle Américaine'
is on her way to Smyrna where,
coincidentally as well,
you meet up with the Zohrabs,
the couple whose remarkable
and well-stocked cellar you helped drain,
whose English books you've given to
that rather stunning princess.
There's no recrimination though.
For reasons that remain unclear
the Zohrabs, holed up here in Smyrna,
still miss their Erzeroum.

Some days at sea, you're back in London
where music halls are dense
with 'patriotic ditties'.
One of them presents
a tableau from the Siege of Plevna.
You're not entirely unimpressed
and offer to the manager
some tips for its improvement.

He tells you that there've been eleven
'veterans' before you who
have likewise claimed that they were there.
You surely find this sort of thing
a trifle disconcerting.
Your Plevna narrative, however,
cannot be complete
without a song of praise for all
the officers and men you served with.
In 1895,
when you are starting on *Red Crescent*,
the murders in Armenia
disfigure all the Melbourne papers.
Even so, your new book notes
the Turkish soldier's 'dauntless courage'
'in earlier and brighter days'.

Hundreds of skulls which had been separated from the bodies were lying there. I thought of the Kurdish colonel, and of the fate which his Circassian servant meted out to the wounded Russian officer, and I guessed the shocking reason. These were the heads of wounded men whom the Circassians had decapitated.

1878, in June,
you're cruising through Port Phillip heads,
up on deck most likely,
staring at the rip;
then searching for the Melbourne skyline,
fire-ladder high back then.

It could be you're with Marian,
your mother, who has been in England
or maybe you're alone.
We have no details of the ship
or what the weather was.
It could have been a clipper but
more probably it's steam.

It's been a good four years since you
set out for Edinburgh
to finish off your course.
The *Wanderjahr*'s turned into three
you couldn't have foreseen.

One can't but wonder re your feelings,
looking north across the bay.
You're far from overwhelmed, I'd reckon;
you've seen too much already.
A life of medicine in Melbourne
will seem a tad sedate,
compared to being shot at
while taking off a leg
or running typhus wards.

Your father Charles, of Ryan & Hammond,
is still well-off and able to
ensure you get your name in brass
as specialist on upper Collins.
The Ryans are not without connections;
your years at Melbourne Grammar
ensure some useful friends.

In all, it shouldn't be too hard.
And, standing at the bow,
you don't quite realise how
you're almost a celebrity.
Letters in the London Times,
as well as in the Melbourne papers,
have praised your work at Plevna;
also your own accounts all through
the Argus six months earlier.
The nickname 'Plevna' now will soon
be frequently applied —
although the Turks began it.
As far as Melbourne is concerned,
with all its fears of 'Rooshuns',
you chose the better side.

The city blocks rise into view;
then Melbourne Port appears.
You'll need a lad to help with luggage.
Your father Charles, we must assume,
is waiting on the wharf
and seriously pleased to see you.
You've been a credit *and* a worry.
You're still just twenty-five and he
is neatly turning sixty.
Your mother, still ten years his junior,
is standing there beside you or ...
impatient on the dock.

The Russians in the redoubt must have reserved their fire, for nearly every man of the first company had five or six bullets through him. The redoubt itself was full of dead and dying men, and the Russians, having rallied, were already coming back beyond their foremost line, being within about five hundred yards of the redoubt. It was plain that if our men did not retire they would be annihilated, and they began to fall back in good order, taking as many of the wounded with them as possible.

You don't take long to get established.
Your fame's preceded you.
A dinner's held at Scott's Hotel
for 'fifty gentlemen' who 'welcome
back their young Victorian
from scenes of bloodshed to
the safety of his friends and colleagues'.
Responding to their lively toast,
you point out that you've never
made a speech before.
And soon are under way to praise
the med school that produced you
(for Edinburgh's Anatomy
you had no further need of books)
and cheerfully concede that you
have been 'exceptionally lucky'
(no argument with that!). You praise
the Stafford House Committee
that sent you off to Erzeroum
and give some fleeting hints on how
the med school and the hospital
might draw a little closer.
You then resume your seat amid
tumultuous applause.

As a surgeon you are fast,
decisive, with a gift for
diagnosis, and the courage
to press on. You're spooked though, just
a little, when, on washing up
for that initial, all-important
operation at Royal Melbourne
you find a theatre dense with colleagues
crowding in to see 'the man
from Plevna' at his work.

Your daughter writes, much later, that
you walked in 'whistling a popular air'.
From all those honorary appointments
gained across the years,
we must presume that all goes well.
Within twelve months you're on the staff
and stay till your 'retirement'
just before the war.

Your private 'rooms', however,
are hardly less important.
Consulting hours are 'twelve till two'.
You join the city's surgeons,
up there at the 'top of Collins',
who call each other 'Mister' lest
their patients think them mere 'physicians'.
Your brass plate's straight across
the road from Parliament,
Cnr Spring and Collins.
You're there for just a few years till
you move across to 37,
opposite the Melbourne Club,
squarely there among your colleagues,
quite a few of whom
are bachelors and still resist
your new-found domesticity.
But first we have that business of
Ned Kelly at Glenrowan.

Our communication with Plevna would no doubt be cut off during the night, and we apprehended that when the morning came our force would probably be annihilated. When day broke, however, we looked out of our stook, and found to our intense relief that there was not a Russian in sight anywhere. It was the most beautiful morning that I remember to have ever seen; and after the bare hills round Plevna and the narrow streets of the town, the well timbered, undulating country was a delightful sight.

You're sent up on the second train,
along with Captain Standish.
They know of your experience
with every sort of wound.
You understand their need, no doubt,
to capture him alive
and then to see him hanged.
It's been a mite embarrassing,
these past three years with what the press
is calling 'Kelly Country'.

There's some confusion in the records
concerning what you do.
You're not the only doctor
restoring Ned to health.
Doctor Nicholson, Benalla,
is first to dress the wounds
and Doctor Shields of Pentridge
gets Ned well enough to hang
without unseemliness.
But you, 'Chas. Ryan', are in the van
that brings him down to Melbourne.
Your interview is in the Argus,
June 30, 1880.

I see you briefing the reporter,
a young man taking notes.
You talk of Ned as speaking 'little'
and how he 'glared at strangers'.
You note his constitution ('splendid')
and how most men, so badly hurt,
would be a good deal more 'prostrated'.
You note Ned's body is
(suspiciously?) 'well nourished'.
He won't say where he got the food.
You think to find him 'very dirty'
but, no, his skin is 'clean' as if
he's had a 'Turkish bath'.

You tell, while coming south by train,
how you 'attended to his wounds'.
He takes some 'brandy' and some 'water'
but you are more than clear
your patient 'wants to die' although
his wounds would not prove mortal in
'an ordinary case'.

The young reporter's keen for more.
You start to list the damage:
left arm with 'two bullet holes',
made, you say, by 'one discharge'.
The right hand and the right leg
contained 'ten slugs' in all.
The ball of one of Ned's big toes
received a 'nasty wound'.
The wound to Ned's 'left groin'
is hardly 'dangerous'.
You note his pulse rate dropped
eleven beats per minute
while in the van to Melbourne.

You've talked with him about the gang.
Joe Byrne, says Ned, was brave enough
to shoot himself and not surrender.
He doubts though that his brother, Dan,
will have the 'pluck' to do so.
Towards the end you tell the Argus
Ned's breath had smelt as if he'd been
'drinking very bad liquor'.

'And how,' the Argus must have asked,
'does Superintendent Hare progress?'
'Getting on well', considering.
'The wound is a very nasty one.'
You flash your Plevna expertise
by noting how the bullet was
'conical', 'revolving at a

very rapid rate'.
You think an amputation
'will not be necessary'.
Hare's been leading the police
and Ned's the murderer.
To you they're just a pair of patients,
requiring expertise.

Every corpse was fearfully disfigured. The faces had been slashed with sabres even after death, and the corpses had been subjected to horrible indignities which are usually supposed to be practised only by the hill tribes of Afghanistan. Whether those atrocities were committed by the Russians or by the Bulgarians I could not definitely determine; but the sight enraged the Circassians to an appalling extent, and their threats boded ill for any Russians who might fall into their hands alive.

By 1883, you're thirty
and well-established now.
Five years, it's been, since you returned;
five years too since those two women,
one at Erzeroum
and one at Istanbul,
the Russian girl (with General)
who maybe still is turning through
the English books you stole;
likewise 'La belle Américaine',
the actress on her honeymoon,
those blue days on the Bosphorus.

You clearly have a taste for women,
the beautiful, intelligent,
and somehow safely married.
It is an age of brothels too.
You talk about Constantinople's
teasing *cafés chantants*
but they were innocent — or fairly.
Your textbooks and your surgery
have shown you more than one could want
of syphilis and gonorrhea.
You know about the mercury,
the methods that don't work,
the Stage III syphilis which brings,
to those who lose their grip on prudence,
insanity then death

The risks you took in battle seem
more sudden and more clean
although you've always relished in
a woman's 'frankness' of expression.

And now, we're told, you want 'nine sons'.
A medico knows how it's done.
At twenty-eight and twenty-nine,

we must assume (no footnotes here)
you start to look around.

The woman you are wanting will
be found through old connections.
Attractive and well-educated
but not so well as you.
She must be upper middle class,
know how to run a household and
retain the loyalty of her staff.
Sensible with money too
since that is not your forte.
You mother, Marian, was just
eighteen when she was married
back there at Killeen.

In ways that we can guess at
but never know for sure
you track down Alice Sumner,
daughter of old Theo Sumner,
merchant, politician, with
a mansion up at Stony Park,
a beach house too at Earimil
not far from Mount Eliza.

She's grown up in that stern
but rather tranquil house although
she's quite a rider and
can happily chase foxes.
Later she will take to driving
but that's some distance off.
You'd be a catch, no doubt;
your humour, too, an asset —
and all those friends who call you 'Charlie'.
You both have cards ... and play them right.

The Charles Ryan/Alice Sumner courtship
leaves no solid traces,
no trails of playful correspondence.
There's just the one certificate.
July 5, 1883,
you're married up at Christ Church, Brunswick.
And who knows what the weather was?

You lease that 'stucco villa'
from Mr Edwin James,
Cnr Spring and Collins,
and start out on a Melbourne marriage
that thrives for forty years.

The roar of the artillery, the rattle of the musketry, the explosion of the shells, the loud hurrahs of the Russians, and the cries of the wounded made up a perfect hell. I met Czetwertinksi near the redoubts, and he and I made renewed efforts to rally the men; but we were powerless to stop the tide of fugitives. Czetwertinski drove the point of his sword into a man's leg without being able to stop him; and at last, as it was getting hotter and hotter, he said to me that it was hopeless stopping there, and we had better be off.

Why is it though that, after Plevna,
you're still have time for soldiering?
We know you always took an interest,
well beyond your contract,
in strategy and tactics,
visiting hard-pressed redoubts
to check how friends were faring.
You had a certain feel for horse-flesh.
Perhaps that sudden, one-off charge,
brandishing a sword and pistol,
sparked a life-long taste
for rushed adrenalin.
As did the scamper back
with bullets all around you.

What is it then that drags you in?
The quality of conversation
on offer in the mess?
That nebulous, late-Empire
duty to the Queen?
A simple yen for uniform?
Arriving home, it's only months
till you're a captain in
Victoria's militia.

It's no coincidence
the photos that we have of you
display your finery.
As does the well-known painting
done by Bernard Hall
which shows the cap and epaulettes,
the military expression
to go with the moustache
which, as your daughter tells us,
would vary with the fashion.
It renders you a little pompous
but that could just be Hall.

The friends to whom you're 'Charlie'
mention always wit and humour.

In 1902, you're made a colonel:
P.M.O., Victoria.
It's all the fibres of a network,
the 'honorary positions',
the high consultancies.
One attainment leads to others.

Not everyone's a friend however.
As C.M.O. for Railways
and later in the A.I.F.
the men you judge still 'fit for work',
the ones you think are 'swinging lead',
can often get quite grouchy.
'Old basket,' one is heard to say.
'If you're warm, you're in.'

When August, '14, comes around
you're almost sixty-one
and speedily appointed
ADMS of First Division,
Birdwood's A.I.F.
October and you're off to Egypt
aboard the 'Orvieto'.

April 25,
you're 'present at the landing',
whatever that may mean exactly,
but let's not go there yet.

At daybreak, I went back to my quarters for a sleep. The Russian batteries had advanced to closer range, and two shells exploded in my garden. A bullet came through the door of the room where I was lying, and buried itself in the wall just before I fell asleep.

And what about domestic life
at 37 Collins?
Not just your surgery's stuffed birds,
the waywardness of stairs and landings,
but all the household servants
your daughter, Maie, remembers
always with affection.
Though that might not apply
to always brisk Miss Jarvis,
'consulting-room attendant',
'wasp-waisted with a wide, dark skirt',
'strong-minded' and efficient.

More congenial to Maie
(whom you have nick-named 'Tom')
are Winifred and Kate, the cooks,
who linger thirty years or so.
And also there's the 'house-boy', James,
who works as 'coachman' too
and stays on when you try to sack him,
deterring applicants.
Later, he will marry
'house-maid' Susan. And die too young
of cancer, just to spite your skills.

Most notable perhaps is Berthe
who comes from Switzerland
supposedly to teach Maie French …
and be an extra mother.

No question Alice is in charge.
She's 'Mrs Ryan', no doubt,
to all the servants cited here.
With James, in your 'Victoria',
she makes her social round,
calling cards with corners turned
to show that she was there in person.

Sometimes Maie (your 'Tom') goes too
and waits outside if friends are 'in'.
At ease in her society,
it's clear that Alice stokes the fire
you first had seen in her.

In 1902, you watch her take
to motoring with some *élan*.
You buy, with her encouragement,
a new de Dion Bouton,
some say the city's first.
It's strong as half a dozen horses.
James, the 'coachman', is the driver
but Alice steers more often
and, everywhere it stops, the car
will guarantee a crowd.
As a firm equestrian
you cannot but distrust it
but finally you come around,
conceding that it's good for business.
You never learn to drive it though,
protesting that it might affect
your surgeon's 'steadiness of hand'.

At weekends it is all your wife's.
With Maie, aged six by her account,
excited in the back,
Alice dons her hat and veil
and often with your friend, Dick Stawell,
heads out for the country.
They boast, on their return, how they
clocked almost 30 m.p.h.
along the road from Dandenong.
'They go much faster,' Alice offers,
'in the evening air'.

The Turks became almost delirious with the excitement of victory. Everywhere men were shouting, praying, and giving thanks to Allah ... The excitement of the five minutes following the recapture of the redoubts was worth a lifetime of commonplace existence; but all the while in the Grivitza redoubt, three miles away, the enemy stood watching with cannons ready — a silent warning of the conflicts yet in store for us.

And what about the children?
In 1883
you and Alice set to work,
enthusiastically
we must surmise. And, right on time,
the first of your intended nine
arrives within the year.
Rupert Sumner Ryan,
1884 to
1952,
Lieutenant–Colonel, M.H.R.,
but that is some way off.

You're living in the 'stucco house',
Cnr Spring & Collins,
where Alice, not much later,
almost dies of typhoid fever.
It sparks the move across the road
to 37 Collins,
a little more salubrious
and blessed with better drains.
We don't know if the two of you
share the nine-fold aspiration
but, either way, it takes eight years
before your daughter, Maie, appears
in 1891.
By then it's clear you've compromised
on just the one of each.

The house, according to your daughter,
is 'difficult' and 'intricate',
not well-suited to its purpose
with bathrooms in odd places and
its stairways 'branched at random'.
The dining room, as Maie remembers,
has a lithograph by Doré
showing the Avenging Angel
expelling Eve and Adam.

The surgery is famous for
your taxidermist's birds,
disconsolate on perches
or sullen under glass.
Many you have stuffed yourself
but not with expertise.
Along with fellow birders
you sponsor expeditions,
one to far away Cape York.
There'd been no stuffing birds at Plevna.

Your daughter claims your textbook shelves
hold for her a sort of strangeness,
their 'paintings of misshapen limbs'
and 'strange diseases' not unlike
a garden of 'exotic flowers'.
And yet the room is cheerful mainly,
patients being set as ease
or joked back into health.

And evenings are more so:
cigars and friends, the trays set out
with food and drink for what you know
as 'yarning'. The thoughts of upper Collins
contending with the world.

Anecdotes and wild opinions.
I wonder if it's in these years
you quell 'the maniac'
who's mentioned in your *obit*,
the one who has a whim to start
'revolver practice in a theatre'.
We're told there how, 'with promptitude
and reckless courage', you leap across
the intervening seats 'to come
to grips with the armed madman'.
A milder Plevna moment
that slips past unrecorded. Almost.

Owing to the continuous nature of the work, I never went back to my quarters during the week after the battle, but used to sleep at the hospital. My Circassian servant cooked my food, such as it was, at my house, and brought it down to me while I was at work. As on the previous occasions, Osman Effendi and myself performed all operations in the open air under a big willow tree on the bank of the Tutchenitza, and in the shadow of an old Turkish mosque, where every evening at sundown an ancient priest, mounting a minaret, called the faithful to prayer.

Knowledge and experience
are not, it's clear, a guarantee
of all one needs re progeny.
Collectively, you're giving all
your energies to Rupert
who shines at every turn.
When it's time you send him off
to Grammar at Geelong.
At fourteen, he's away to Harrow
and, in due course, becomes
'head boy on the modern side'.
Later, he'll check into Woolwich
Military Academy
and make a clean sweep there,
'passing out' in 1904.
In her memoir, Maie will wonder
what the cost to you and Alice
must have really been,
banishing your only son
so early from your lives.

She herself remembers Rupert
only twice in Collins Street
although they draw much closer
following the war.
In *An Australian Story*
(London, 1962)
it's clear Maie feels she suffered
rather less than Rupert did
from all that spiritual rigour
the British upper middle class
habitually imposed
(though these are not her words).

By 1914, Rupert's in
the Royal Artillery.
By war's end he's been wounded once,

is six times 'mentioned in dispatches'
and sports a D.S.O.
To 'Plevna' Ryan that's no small thing.
Afterwards, in 1920,
he's on the Rhineland High Commission's
HQ at Coblenz,
checking on the Germans.
And surely it is touching
that 'Coblenz' is the place of death
in Alice's obituary —
1923.

Sadly, you don't live to see
how Rupert, top-flight soldier,
retires in '29,
sells arms for Vickers Ltd,
becomes a sort of British spy,
returns to run a stud at Berwick,
in 1940 wins the seat
of Flinders for the U.A.P.,
serves on numerous committees
and dies in '52.
He, like you, was popular.
And well-regarded in the Reps
across the 'Great Divide'
for 'kindliness and tolerance'.

In 1926,
off Adelaide and dying,
you probably foresee as much.

He was holding some object in his hand, and his appearance was so strange that I went over and had a look at him. I found that he had been shot in the abdomen, and about two feet of the small intestine had prolapsed, and was protruding through the wound. It was so altered in appearance by exposure that it looked exactly like a bit of tarred rope.

Maie (or 'Tom', as you prefer)
is quite a different story.
She's not the nine you have in mind;
an eight-year gap between two births
suggests some complication.
You find though that she has your spark;
is curious and fearless.
Her 'large blue eyes and delicate skin'
are universally admired.
Both you and Alice, that first year,
are seriously amused
with how her cries across the street
distress the bachelors,
holed up in the Melbourne Club.

At four or five, Maie's brought with you
touring through the wards.
She notices they're glad to see you
but finds the whole thing disconcerting.
'Terror and distaste' she writes,
recalling it at seventy.
You also walk with her down Collins
for special ice creams at
the Café de Paris.

Berthe, the maid from Switzerland,
sees her much more often;
takes her down to Coles' Arcade
and, though she is a 'governess',
shares your daughter's room.
Plainly, she's kind of 'nanny'
though no one calls her that.
The two of them grow very close.

And sometimes you will call 'Tom' in
to heal a patient with her cuteness.
And sometimes when there are no clients
she turns the pages of your texts

and you don't take them from her.
She's almost always there at lunch,
your table set for six in case
a friend or colleague should 'drop in'
as they very often do.
And sometimes there are relatives:
Granny Ryan, already deaf,
your sister, Ellis Rowan,
the painter who knows plants the way
that you aspire to birds.

Aged sixteen, your 'Tom' is sent
to boarding school at Ascot; then
to Paris to be 'finished'.
Your good friend, Richard Stawell
(the motorist), advises that
the university's no good
for girls and tells of how at Cambridge
his sister had a 'breakdown'.

While you are at Gallipoli
and, later on, in London
Maie volunteers to work
with wounded officers in Melbourne
and, when hostilities are over,
you're happy she can 'hostess'
for Rupert in Coblenz.

In 1924 in London
she meets again with Richard Casey,
known to her from childhood.
In June of '26,
four months before your death,
they're married at St James, Westminster
and here the story ends
as far as you're concerned.

A brace of Casey children
arrive a few years on,
'28 and '31.
You don't know that your son-in-law
becomes the Member for Corio
and Treasurer in '35,
Ambassador to Washington
in 1940, kicked aside,
it's often said, by Menzies who
spoke of Maie as 'Macbeth's wife'.

'Macbeth', with no great ruthlessness,
is chosen by the British as
their wartime Bengal governor.
It's hard to know what you'd have thought
of all the things your daughter does,
the writing, painting, or
to see her piloting a Cessna.

In 1960, Dick's a baron
and Maie's his baroness.
In '65, Bob Menzies on
the cusp of his retirement gives
your son-in-law his final gig,
the house at Yarralumla.
For women of her time and class,
you'd happily concede, Maie's was
a notable achievement;
indirect, vicarious,
but real as any other.

One man came under my hands who received six wounds from one bullet. The ball struck him on the outside of the right arm between the elbow and the shoulder, passed through the arm, through the fleshy portions of the chest, and through the left arm as well, leaving six distinct bullet-holes, all of which I washed and plugged. He made a rapid recovery, and after a few weeks in the hospital went back to the trenches.

I like the thought of all that 'yarning',
with just a whiff of brandy and a
flourish of cigars.
It's said that there is singing too;
your voice a baritone,
'pleasant', 'light', inclined towards
an Irish melody.
It can't be just 'Men Only' but
the males must dominate.

Dr Helen Sexton,
respected medico,
turns up now and then.
And Alice, no doubt, holds her own,
'more at ease with men than women'.
And curled up in a chair
or reading on the floor,
young Maie's acquiring quite enough
to write a chapter decades on.
Anything is much more fun
than early off to bed.

Dick Stawell and Felix Myer are
two good friends whom she remembers.
Hamilton Russell is another;
authority on antiseptics,
who sometimes plays piano.
A 'dreamy man', by Maie's account.
Only you and Hamilton
are close enough to call her 'Tom'.
In 1926 he'll be
the one entrusted with the task
of writing your obituary.
He'll talk of how your 'friends
were cosmopolitan' and how
you had 'a genius for friendship';
adding, just to set things straight,

how 'one was always laughing with him
or smiling at him' (quietly?).

Maie's fond of Dr Stawell as well
and wears no grudge in retrospect
about the poor advice
he gave you re the 'Varsity'
and how it's bad for women.
Felix Myer's more exotic,
a gynaecologist.
You and he are champions
for letting women into Med
back in 1887.

Roughly twice a week you hold them,
these colloquies with bachelors.
And some of them, of course,
are more than charmed by Alice —
the way you were in Erzeroum
 by that young Russian princess and
'*La belle Américaine*', beguiled
by what you couldn't have.

Among these happy conversants
 there would have been as well
the Irish journalist, John Sandes,
ten years younger than yourself,
'Oxford man', also a poet,
writing for the Argus,
reviewing music and the theatre.
Later he would publish five
quite popular collections
that nailed the 'spirit of the age',
including *Landing in the Dawn*
(1916). Also novels.

No doubt, 'yarning' in the '90s,
he'd hear, with suitable amazement,

your anecdotes of Plevna
and tales of Erzeroum —
and badger you to write them down.
Do you offer to dictate them
or does he just do final 'tunings'?
Or add, perhaps, 'poetic touches'?
Your preface says he 'brightened' things
but always left the truth
'absolutely unimpaired'.
Your letters sent from Plevna
and published in the Argus are
another source. It's interesting
that you and Sandes do not re-run
the bit where you confess (or brag?)
'I shot a Russian soldier dead',
though plainly it's in self-defence.
The Plevna letters, by design,
with Melbourne audience in mind,
rejoice in tactics and adventure
and, strangely for a surgeon, are
more strategy than scalpel.
Both names though are on the spine
of what John Murray gave the world
in London, 1897.

Perhaps young Sandes does typing only.
There's so much, right throughout the book,
that only you, Charles, could have written.
It's all too graphic, of a piece,
to think your Irish friend does more
than burnishing a phrase or two.
It's notable that you, not he,
are present at Gallipoli
and take part, more or less,
in what he calls the Landing.
Of interest, too, that little Maie
does not recall him at the 'yarnings'.
You like to talk to journalists

(see the cameo re Ned)
and, further back, you get on well
with all those 'foreign correspondents'
writing up their wild accounts
of derring-do at Plevna.

Certainly the odour from the ill fated corpses, both of the Turks and of their so gallant and courageous assailants, was decidedly offensive; but it would not be fair to allow the Russians to incur the whole of the annoyance which would attach to the burial of so many patriots who had fallen on the field of honour. In effect he would propose as an alternative that if the Russians would inconvenience themselves to the extent of sending out a party of men to bury all the corpses within ninety yards of their redoubt, the Turks on their side would feel it a pleasure and an honour to bury all the bodies within a similar distance of the work which they occupied. Thus the labour would be equally divided and the interment carried out most satisfactorily.

So, no, you don't forget the Turks.
Nor the Russians either.
For thirty years you're following,
via the Argus and the Age,
and London Times (weeks later),
the way allegiances are shifting
and how the Germans take the role
that Britain once assumed
back there in the Plevna days.
It saddens you, no doubt.

You also act as Melbourne's
'honorary Turkish Consul',
a role approved of by the Queen.
You keep your Turkish up a bit
by speaking it at 'Tom'
or with a tiny handful
of Melbourne Turks back then.

It isn't always comfortable.
In 1895
the pogroms in Armenia
are splashed all through the Melbourne press.
A column in the Argus pokes
considerable fun at you
for drumming up a trade between
Victoria and Istanbul,
surmising that the Turk
('unspeakable') and fresh
from certain massacres
may choose to clothe himself in tweeds
appropriately woven by
the 'Giaours of Geelong'.
You share but also slowly shed
your Empire's fear of Russia.

Revisiting your 'youthful exploits',
you're in Constantinople when

the 'Young Turks' come to power
or just a few days later.
The revolution's 'marvellous',
you offer in an interview
when landing back in Perth. You tell
your interlocutor that 'only
one man was assassinated'
and plausibly recount the way
it starts in Macedonia
with officers ashamed
to front their European
counterparts while dressed in 'rags',
their 'pay embezzled by'
a slew of Ottoman officials.
The crowds you've seen in Istanbul
carry on like 'schoolboys',
so great is their 'delight'.
Your loyalty to the Sultan is
a little less than absolute.

You note also the growing fuss
about the Berlin–Baghdad Railway.
You see the 'British perfidy'
when battleships for Turkey are
abruptly 'requisitioned',
the Germans stepping in with two
'convenient' replacements.
Two days before the war begins
the Turks and Germans sign a pact,
a secret one, unknown to Melbourne.
Three months later, more or less,
October 27,
Turkey joins the Central Powers
against the Great Entente
and promptly sends a little fleet
to bombard Russian warships
anchored in Odessa.

By now, we know, you have 'retired',
are working as 'consultant' only.
Your last day at the RMH
leaves us a description of
your final operation
and how, while waiting for
a slow anaesthetist,
you finished a cigar;
then flicked it in a bucket.

From 1902 you've been a colonel,
voluntary militia,
When war's declared you're suddenly
A.D.M.S., appointed to
the First Division, A.I.F.
and, by October, you're at sea
for Egypt where you join the staff
of General Sir William Birdwood.

Hard to know exactly what
your troopship thoughts would be.
Worry, no doubt, over Rupert
in the Royal Artillery;
and Maie, a little less,
at twenty-three a volunteer
(with no especial training)
back home helping with the wounded,
lieutenants and above.

You'd also muse on Turkish friends
at Erzeroum and Plevna,
rather less long-lived than you
you'd reasonably presume.
It's not clear yet where you are headed.
Most probably the Western Front —
the Dardanelles as yet
a dream on Churchill's pillow.

I often paid a visit to the Bash Tabiva in the afternoon to have a cup of coffee and a cigarette with old Sadik Pasha, who was in command, and these afternoon calls were always attended with a certain amount of risk. The fellows in the Grivitza redoubt used to keep a look out for visitors; but the range was over eight hundred yards, and I used to skip across those thirty yards of exposed space, dodging like a strong blue rock before the barrels of the pigeon-shooter, and always coming through safely. It did not take me more than three seconds to cover the distance, and before they could sight their rifles I was across.

In Egypt, it's a long five months,
waiting on the British winter
and 'guarding the Canal'.
Although you're high on Birdwood's staff
you surely must be seeing patients,
Australians and New Zealanders,
those cheery volunteers,
catching what they shouldn't when
they're cutting loose in Cairo.
The term they use is 'larrikin'
when diggers think they've been short-changed
by certain 'dens of ill-repute'.
Then, finding a more docile mood,
they check the pyramids at Giza
and have their photos taken.
No doubt, you take a few yourself,
that handy little Jules Richard,
the 45 x 107.
You like to have things up to date
and are an early devotee
of photographs in colour.

I wonder too if these
decidedly impatient ANZACS
turn your thoughts to all those wild
Circassians at Plevna,
so disinclined to prisoners
and expert at marauding.
But that may not be fair.
These soldiers, fresh from Melbourne and
Victoria's small towns,
these youthful, blithe adventurers
from all around the country,
are not unlike yourself perhaps
before you went to Widdin.
A sort of innocence attends them.

But you know what they're soon to learn
when news comes through of Churchill's scheme
and suddenly you're off to Lemnos.

At almost sixty-one,
you're wondering why you've come.
Young men in their early twenties;
boys, sixteen, who've upped their age.
Even your commander
checks in at twelve years younger.
But duty, as you know, is duty
and Alice, back in Melbourne,
can manage well enough alone
or with her band of servants.
And Maie is there as well.
You're not so chuffed to face the Turks though.
You wear their medals still.
There's no doubt though that doctors,
and ones of your experience,
will be in sharp demand
when longboats hit the beach.

I went back into the redoubt, and dressed the Nubian's heel. Then the Turkish major and I had coffee and cigarettes together, and I gave him the ointment for his chin, whereat he was much gratified. We were so much accustomed to whole hecatombs of victims in those days, that we were callous to a single casualty.

'At the Landing,' sources say,
but what's that mean exactly?
You're too high up for 'crack of dawn'
and splashing through the waves.
You're there to see them leave the transports,
off into that late-night darkness,
the cliffs unseen, their shadows felt;
though soon enough, you come ashore,
aboard the 'Minnesota'.
'A little after eight' is what
you tell the Dardanelles Commission
in 1917.

We have that photo of you still,
relaxed outside a dug-out,
leaning back against the sandbags,
jodhpurs, leggings, shirt sleeves, tie.
A sign says 'A.D.C.'.
You're just a little paunchy
and generously moustached.
The smile is wry but comfortable.
It must be weeks now since the landing
and things have settled down a bit.
It's probably before that truce,
just short of one month in,
on May the 24th.

Is any of the chaos yours?
The Casualty Clearing Stations,
despite the shellfire on the beach,
perform 'exceptionally well'
in your opinion but
you're mainly on the transports
acting now as 'hospitals'
standing three miles out.
Ten of them you're on in all,
doing what you can
with what's been not supplied.

One of them's without a single
bed pan so the wounded men
must 'defæcate in their breaches'.
Another has no nurses.
You don't sell nurses short.
In that postwar interview,
you cite the case of Sister Marshall
who works for weeks on end,
9 a.m. to 3 next morning.
'A more capable woman,' you insist,
'I've never come across'.

The 'Luxor' is a 'beastly boat',
a 'filthy thing', you later tell
the Dardanelles Commission.
The 'Gascon' straight from India
is notably more 'pukka'.
It's never just administration;
'One morning I did five
amputations before breakfast'.
'A slick ... well-practised amputator,'
is what they say in Melbourne.
You're both 'consulting' and 'on call';
and working solidly at both,
though not, it seems, the slow repairs
attempted back at Lemnos.

Those first few days the 'medical
evacuations' don't go well.
Casualties on this scale have
never been envisaged,
though knowing what you saw at Plevna
no doubt you could have told them.
One ship supplied for surgery
is ankle deep in horse-dung.
Another still has horses on it,
two hundred, you recall,

all night kicking in their stalls.
The risk of tetanus is high.

In London, two years on,
you're telling the commission
of shortfalls they're not keen to hear.
You dwell on maladministration that
at one stage tossed some eighty tons
of fresh beef overboard.

Six days before the truce
you're not there when your general
is picked off by a sniper through
the 'femoral artery'.
He takes two days to die. You tell
your future son-in-law, Dick Casey,
the general's aide-de-camp,
that probably you could have saved him
had you been near to hand.

As an officer you'd wear
a handy Webley on your belt
but surely now, at sixty-one,
your nippings-off-to-check-the-fight
would be less frequent than
they used to be at Plevna.
General Bridges was another
who liked to get too close.

On May 19, pre-dawn,
the Turks begin their mass attack,
designed to drive the ANZACs
back into the sea.
In darkness and first light,
Vickers and Lee-Enfields
slow their wild advance.
In just six hours, those bullets leave
four thousand Turkish dead.

Most of them are in a wheat field.
The Turks have come with full equipment,
rolled blankets and entrenching tools,
intending to acquire some ground
and stay a week or two.
In the morning someone says,
peering from a firestep, the whole
thing looks for just a moment
'like a field of sleeping men'.

Five days go by; it's almost summer.
The stench that's always been inherent
becomes impossible.
A white flag and a blindfold
begin negotiations.
A nine-hour truce to stop the smell:
Turkish dead, a few Australians,
New Zealanders as well.
Some have been there for a month,
killed on that first day.

May 24, 0730,
men from both sides equally
clamber from their trenches
and, bearing spades and shovels,
enter 'no man's land'.
They pause awhile, exchanging
'cigarettes and souvenirs'.
Some officers on either side
talk French as best they can.
The ease with which they fraternise
might well alarm a home M.P.
if he were brave enough to visit.

As medico in charge,
it's only right you supervise,
directing the interments.

These bodies, sprawled and rotting,
are hazardous to health
and dysentery is rife already.
You walk among the corpses,
quietly giving orders.
The shovel parties overlap;
and now some Turkish officers
have seen your Plevna decorations.
They think, like some Circassian,
you stole them from the dead
and start to remonstrate.
'No, no,' you say in Turkish.
'I got these when I fought at Plevna
with Gazi Osman Pasha.'
And then, we're told, they're hugging you
expansively as comrades.

Soon though, it is back to work,
burying four thousand dead
and more in just nine hours.
And no one seems to mind too much
when you get out your Jules Richard
and take those sepias of the scene
that circulate today.
Bloated bodies, middle-distance;
men resting on their spades.
The earth looks hard but friable;
the graves, we must suppose,
are not as deep as those
in Melbourne's General Cemetery
where you, with your 'three score
and ten' — plus three — will end at last.

4:30 in the afternoon,
the Red Cross and Red Crescent flags
are taken down reluctantly.
A few last jokes are swapped.

Captain Aubrey Herbert
afterwards recalls:
'I joked with them in Turkish how
they'd try to shoot me the next day
and they returned, in chorus, with
"God forbid. We will never shoot you." '

The whole campaign's got seven more
corrosive months to run
but you'll be free in June.

Now the specific charm of the mortar is that it throws a shell with a very high trajectory, so that the projectile can soar like a hawk into the heavens and swoop down perpendicularly upon its prey. With all their ingenuity the Turks had not succeeded in devising a protection from this mode of annoyance; and as the Turkish soldier was coming along like a well drilled waiter with a tray on his arm containing three cups of coffee, the mortar-shell exploded in the redoubt. No one was killed, but a fragment of the casing knocked the tray and the cups and saucers into smithereens, and Sadik Pasha had to order "The same again, please."

'Enteric Fever', 'Dysentery';
you know the symptoms well
from back at Erzeroum.
A few days from that nine-hour truce
you feel it coming on:
the cough, the temperature and headache,
the green, 'pea soup' diarrhoea
that has a special stink,
the segue to delirium,
the worry of a perforation.
At one point, you're reported dead
but you know what the trouble is;
you're simply lying low.
Your deep-down British sense of duty
does not allow for doubt

but finally you can't go on.
They send a telegram to Alice
that you are 'dangerously ill'.
You're boated to a transport
floating out of range
and thence to Alexandria
and Cairo where, with bowel restored,
you're shipped, with three months' leave,
to higher things in London.

And as it was at Plevna,
you don't feel good about the friends
you've had to leave behind.
You're probably not sure
your 2-I-C can do as well
but, somewhere, somehow, you're relieved
to be no longer shot at.
The chances now that Alice,
worried back in Melbourne by
the crackle of that telegram,
will see you once again
are notably improved.

Same goes for daughter Maie.
And possibly those ageing patients,
missing you at 37.

Despite a tussle with a burglar,
two days from your arrival,
it's bracing to be back in London,
centre of the whole shebang —
though now a little drained, of course,
by what's across the Channel.
The Western Front, you know, is not
some larger Russo-Turkish fray.
The killing's turned industrial.
'Adventure' is a word long dead.
The cavalry is obsolete;
although you'll read about Beersheba
with not a little interest.
In London, you're Consulting Surgeon
H.Q., A.I.F.
Horseferry Road. You're also on
a run of those review boards where
you quickly reinforce
your Melbourne reputation
for coming down on bludgers.
All the sources mention it
but what, exactly, do they mean?
It's not just 'bad-back' railway slackers
complaining of a pain
and hoping for a desk.
And how much do you see of what's
becoming known as 'shell-shock'?
Do you talk with Dr Rivers
who's expert on these things,
who treated Owen and Sassoon,
the poets, at Craiglockhart?
Do you peer at twitching limbs
and see a true destruction?

Or do you summon up the Turks
at Plevna, their fortitude beneath
the weight of Russian guns?
One board assesses officers:
you're surely more severe with those
'who just can't take it any more',
young men rich in Greek and Latin
who feared white feathers more than bullets —
or thought they did at first.
You make the big decisions,
impartially we're always told:
'fit for duty' or a ship
to take the damage home.

Promotions, decorations
keep on coming through.
Surgeon General, A.I.F.
in 1917.
An O.B.E. plus several
'mentions in despatches'.

It's not the same as Melbourne but
it has its compensations.
No doubt you find (but we've no proof)
a bolt-hole like the Melbourne Club
with decent conversation and
a nip of single malt,
though most of your good friends, it seems,
recall you as 'abstemious'.
You're missing Alice, missing Maie,
but isn't everyone somehow?
You worry too re Rupert,
out there under heavy guns
a major now and 'mentioned
(six times) in despatches',
finally with D.S.O.

We must assume for those three years
that London offers no diversions —
or nothing that would trouble Alice.
If someone does, she's harmless
and probably well-married.
Duty is Duty, we conclude
all across the board.
In your *obit*, Hamilton
declares you'd 'travel by no road
that was not rigidly straight.'

You're still there at the Armistice:
eleventh hour, eleventh day,
eleventh month — but not,
thank God, eleventh year.
Not even you could handle that.

1919 brings the knighthood
and, in the middle of that year,
the A.I.F. 'retires' you as
an honorary major-general.
You're now 'unfit for service' since
a Harley Street opinion notes
'pain of an anginal nature' and
a heart 'considerably enlarged'.

So now, at last, you're off to Melbourne,
back to Alice, back to Maie,
while Rupert's set to stay in Europe,
high up on the Inter-Allied
Rhineland High Commission.

Five years it's been since Alice
saw you off at Princes Pier
and here you are again,
you just short of 66
and she just 61.

Your wharf-side kisses are just two
of scores of thousands swapped
by veterans and waiting women
trying to retrieve the years.

Some sources say, despite your heart,
you take on several former patients
back at 37.
The 'yarnings' though are not much mentioned.
Young bachelors in wartime
tend not to go the distance.
There is that other 'Big Divide':
those who 'Went' and those who 'Didn't',
each injured in his different way.
One has to think how Alice now
will scarcely find it easy.
Five years' independence; then
her 'Charlie' round the house again.
There would be compensations though,
secret dealings in the sheets
that we've no right to know.

They lay on the floor of the passages as well as in the rooms, and were packed so closely that it was most difficult to pick one's way through the hospital without treading on them. In one room, fifteen feet by fifteen feet, I had sixteen men, all hideously wounded, dying hard on the hard boards. The bare, whitewashed walls were splashed with blood, which had turned to rusty dark brown stains, and the horrors of the place can only be faintly hinted at.

From here on in, it's all denouement;
the sources don't have much to say.
You've had your wars and your promotions;
you've got your decorations;
a knighthood at the finish
to brighten your decline.
They call you in from time to time
to offer an opinion.
It's hard to think, at any age,
that Charlie Ryan could lose momentum.

1919, Great War won,
other endings trim the edges.
It's only four years now till Alice,
at Coblenz on a windy night,
will die at 65
while visiting your 'splendid boy'.

Are you there beside the bed?
It seems that Maie is present.
Or are you back in Melbourne with
'some urgent business to attend to'?
Alice's obituary
suggests perhaps the latter.
'A private cable message was
received in Melbourne yesterday.'
The illness isn't named.

Either way, these days, it's clear
that Europe's on your mind.
Maie, we know, has moved to London
in 1923;
Rupert's in the Rhineland
until the Occupation ends.

In June of '26
your daughter is a British bride
and marries R.G. Casey.

Earlier that year you take
'a holiday in Spain with Maie';
you're very fussed about the wedding,
the organising and the payment.
It's obvious you're there,
St James' Parish Church, Westminster,
to give your 'Tom' away.
And surely you approve of Casey,
ANZAC lad with solid kin,
though not perhaps as tough as you?
Or Maie, come down to that.

Back in 1924
you've sailed to Germany to see
your war-distinguished Rupert married
to Lady Rosemary, aged twenty,
daughter of the Earl of Errol.
Do you diagnose the marriage
will last for just eleven years
and Rupert sail back home
when you are nine years gone?

September now in '26,
the English wedding done with style,
you're sailing home from London on
the R.M.S. 'Otranto',
curving round the globe to Melbourne.
A sea voyage is no sort of problem.
You've always thrived on hardship.
No doubt, you are invited
to join the Captain's table
and, though a knighthood guarantees it,
your anecdotes, goodwill and humour
ensure a place as well.
The captain's suite is like a club:
decent conversation;
cheroots and port most probably
following dessert,

the three-year absence now of Alice
not a worry in this context
though surely there's an edge of loss.

We have no details of the voyage
except, October 23,
8:30 in the morning,
the ship just short of Adelaide,
you suddenly, though not
without presentiment, are ill
and understand at once that it's
a cardiac infarction.
'The surgeon of the ship is summoned'.
You tell your fellow voyagers
there's nothing to be done
and that, in twenty minutes,
you'll probably be dead.
Not unlike a Turk at Plevna,
you wince and bear the pain.
The new-found friends who crowd around you,
their breakfast not long finished,
are sad but not surprised to see
your life's last diagnosis prove
unerringly correct.

One of them, with his strong aquiline face and piercing eyes, reminded me very much of a statue of Dante which I had seen in the market-place of Verona. My patient had been shot through the thigh. The bone had been dreadfully smashed, and the whole leg was a mass of gangrened flesh. If I could have operated, I might have saved his life; but without antiseptic dressings, and without the possibility of subsequent careful nursing, an operation was out of the question, and I had to watch him suffering day by day dying literally by inches.

The body's sent by train to Melbourne.
Your funeral is 'State', of course.
October 27.
The Sydney Morning Herald cites
'A special service in St Paul's ...
attended by a large
and representative gathering'.
The 'Naval, Military and Air Boards'
ensure their thoughtful delegates
are present in their pews.
There are, as well, the medicos
and not a few old patients;
plus those genealogies
that still prevail in Melbourne.
You've died an Anglican despite
your Catholic-sounding name.
It's less than ten years since the War
and service ribbons, serried medals,
are naturally on show.
You *are* a Major-General,
we hardly need reminding.
We almost hear the dean,
more probably the state's archbishop,
intoning mandatory nouns;
words like 'Love' and 'Duty'
liberally scattered.
Your 'yarning' mates (or those remaining),
remembering your laughter,
are not inclined to contradict.
They let it go through to the keeper.

Today at Melbourne Central,
the graveside might be 'family only'
but, no, we're told the gathering
is 'very large'. It's as befits
an eminent Sir Charles — and 'Charlie'
We can be certain Maie and Rupert
aren't there at the grave.

The five-day gap between your death
and notable interment
does not allow a rush from Europe.
Maie, indeed, does not return
till 1931;
Rupert four years later.

Who else is standing by the grave
is difficult to know.
Your sister, Ellis, famous painter,
has died four years before.
The grandchildren are yet to come
or stationed in Coblenz.
And, anyway, in your time, kids
aren't seen at such events.
Some sisters of your own,
some sisters of your wife,
will probably be there
and some pretending to much closer
ties than are the case.
A knighthood tends to bring that on.

A few will say that you've not been
'the same since Alice died'.
And some suggest that it's a shame
your children are both back in Europe
but that's the way it is.
The padré winds things up at last:
'Earth to earth, ashes to ashes …'
but you hear none of it,
the sod sounds on your coffin lid
are in no way distinguished.

And much less do you catch the words
that I have written here
across these past six months or so,
sorting through your book and Maie's
and random slips of evidence

the internet preserves,
managing the clash of dates,
the multiple accounts,
the various lacunae,
the several contradictions
that hinder and release,
forcing one to speculate
while falsifying nothing.

'Maudlin to address the dead',
I argued on p. 1
but even so these lines that trace
a half-year's one-way conversation
have been a slow, accretive pleasure.

I know that I have been to Plevna.
And sometimes too, Charles Ryan,
I've heard you talking back.

As I walked past them up the path the sight of those dead faces fascinated me; and when I found among them men who were my special favourites, and who had told me the stories of their wives and children waiting for them in distant parts of the Turkish Empire, a feeling of overpowering depression came over me. I was so utterly helpless to save them, and I was fighting such a hopeless battle, that once or twice I sat down in the hospital and cried like a child.

Appendix

Quotations from Charles S. Ryan & John Sandes, *Under the Red Crescent: Adventures of an English Surgeon with the Turkish Army at Plevna and Erzeroum, 1877–1878* (John Murray, London, 1897)

1.	p. 31
2.	p. 93
3.	p. 96
4.	p. 123
5.	p. 124
6.	p. 130
7.	p. 133
8.	p. 137
9.	pp. 144–145
10.	p. 147
11.	p. 153
12.	pp. 162–163
13.	p. 172
14.	p. 173
15.	p. 174
16.	p. 179
17.	p. 181
18.	p. 187
19.	p. 188
20.	p. 202
21.	pp. 208–209
22.	p. 213
23.	p. 231

24.   pp. 232–233

25.   p. 236

26.   pp. 239–240

27.   p. 240

28.   p. 241

29.   p. 253

30.   pp. 255–256

31.   p. 257

32.   pp. 268–269

33.   pp. 272–273

34.   pp. 274–275

35.   p. 279

Acknowledgements

This verse biography is based on:

Charles S. Ryan & John Sandes, *Under the Red Crescent: Adventures of an English Surgeon with the Turkish Army at Plevna and Erzeroum, 1877–1878* (John Murray, London, 1897).

Maie Casey, *An Australian Story, 1837–1907* (Michael Joseph, London, 1962).

Maie Casey, 'Charles Snodgrass Ryan', Medical Journal of Australia, September 1959, pp. 390–393.

'Obituary: Charles Snodgrass Ryan', Medical Journal of Australia, November 27, 1926, pp. 746–748.

Other crucial information was also derived from the *Australian Dictionary of Biography* article on Ryan (by Frank M. C. Forster) and a number of other websites which provided excerpts from the *Age*, the *Argus* and other newspapers.

Thanks are also due to Manning Clark House which mounted, in April 2014, the exhibition of Ryan's Gallipoli photographs which originally sparked my interest. Sebastian Clark was also an early reader of the manuscript and offered valuable suggestions.

Thanks should also be made to Robert Nichols, Peter Stanley and Vicken Babkenian and the staffs at the Australian War Memorial Library and the State Library of Victoria for assistance with research.

I also thank my partner, Alison Hastie, for her painstaking proofreading and essential support — and the Australian Defence Force Academy where I have been an honorary visiting fellow for many years.

Image credits
All images courtesy of the Australian War Memorial and taken by Charles Snodgrass Ryan.

Cover images
H00483, an unidentified soldier, standing on a fire step, using a periscope to see outside the trench he is standing in, on the ridge of Lone Pine. A kit bag and water bottle is on a ledge to his right and his Enfield rifle is leaning against the trench in front of him. Note that you can see the image of No Man's Land in the viewer of the periscope, cropped. P01732.001, ANZAC area (Gallipoli). C.1915–07. Various dugouts on the side of the hill including one used as the field post office. (Original colour lantern slide housed in AWM Archive Store (Donor A. Anderson), cropped.

p. 4 Gallipoli Peninsula, Turkey. c May 1915. Australian bivouacs in the gully at Cape Helles. Note the donkeys tethered beside the path on the right. This is one half of a stereo image. The full image is held at P02648.009. (Donor R. G. Casey) P02648.027.

p. 29 Mena, Egypt. c 1915. A general view of Mena Camp through the tent lines, showing pyramids in the background. The tents were all bell tents and at right is a guards tent and a rifle rack beside it. A soldier stands on duty, with his rifle at the slope. Note that the rifle has a bayonet fixed to it. This is one half of a stereo image. The full image is held at C05278A. C05278.

p. 58 Gallipoli Peninsula, Turkey. 24 May 1915. Australian burial parties burying dead Australian and Turkish soldiers at the Nek during the armistice. More than 3,000 Turks and approximately 160 Australians were killed in the Turkish attack on 19 May 1915. Approximately one million rounds of ammunition were fired during the one day attack. The stench from the dead became so unbearable that the Turks initiated a nine hour armistice so that both sides could recover and bury their dead. Note the men wearing red cross armbands. Surgeon General Charles Ryan contravened the terms of the armistice by taking this photograph. This is one half of a stereo image. The full image is held at P02648.007. (Donor R. G. Casey) P02648.025.

p. 83 Gallipoli Peninsula, Turkey. c May 1915. Officers and soldiers conferring in a trench reinforced with sandbags on one of the ridges at Gallipoli. Note the latrine set into an alcove in the wall of the trench. This is one half of a stereo image. The full image is held at P02648.008. (Donor R. G. Casey) P02648.026.

p. 109 Gallipoli Peninsula, Turkey. c May 1915. Surgeon General Sir Charles S. Ryan sitting outside his dugout (marked M.O. for Medical Officer). Surgeon General Ryan was the Medical Officer on Lieutenant General Sir William Riddell Birdwood's staff. This is one half of a stereo image. The full image is held at P02648.011. (Donor R. G. Casey) P02648.029.

p. 130 Gallipoli Peninsula, Turkey. c May 1915. Two soldiers of the Supply Depot, 1st Australian Division, standing on the beach amongst boxes of corned beef and canned meat. Rows of either petrol or water cans are in the foreground. This is one half of a stereo image. The full image is held at P02648.012. (Donor R. G. Casey) P02648.030.

p. 139 Gallipoli Peninsula, Turkey. c May 1915. Lieutenant G. Chirnside standing at Plugge's Plateau. In the background is either Courtney's or Quinn's Post. Note the zigzagged pathways through the terraces on the hill to the right and the trench lines on the hill to the left. This is one half of a stereo image. The full image is held at P02648.006. (Donor R. G. Casey) P02648.024.

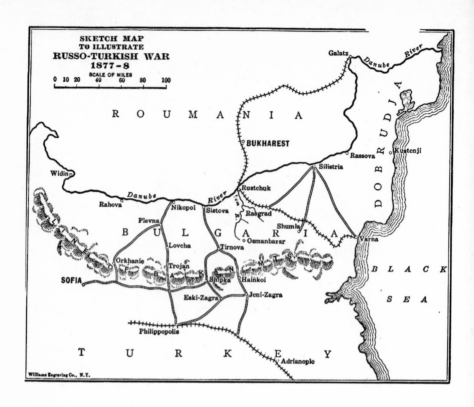

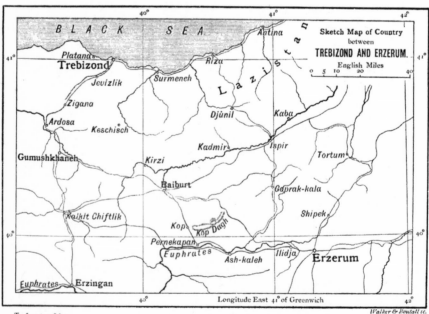